THE POWER OF
THE
A4s

Plate 2: No. 60027 *Merlin* pounds through Hadley Wood station in the north London suburbs with the down 'Capitals Limited' in July 1952. Timed to leave King's Cross at 9.35 am this express ran non-stop to Edinburgh in a little over seven hours and, as with the majority of the east coast premier trains, was usually entrusted to a Gresley Class A4 Pacific.

Previous Page:
Plate 1: A Sunday morning express for Hull and Bradford is lifted up Holloway Bank towards Finsbury Park in north London in September 1953 with No. 60026 *Miles Beevor* showing the effect of the tough adverse gradient and eleven well-laden coaches.

THE POWER OF THE

THE

A4s

by Brian Morrison

Oxford Publishing Co

First published 1978
Reprinted 1984, 1987 and 1988
This impression 2002

ISBN 0 86093 032 7

Published by Oxford Publishing Co

an imprint of Ian Allan Publishing Ltd, Hersham, Surrey KT12 4RG.
Printed by Ian Allan Printing Ltd, Hersham, Surrey KT12 4RG.

Code: 0203/3

INTRODUCTION

It was September 1966 when the reign of Sir Nigel Gresley's Class A4 Pacifics officially came to an end with the withdrawal of Nos. 60019 *Bittern* and 60024 *Kingfisher* from the stock list of the Scottish Region of British Rail. It was almost exactly 31 years before that the first of the class had been introduced by the LNER to work the new streamlined 'Silver Jubilee' express from King's Cross to Newcastle. In the years intervening the locomotives were to become the most famous of all types on LNER and Eastern Region metals and many would say the most famous of any locomotives ever built in this country.

Within three weeks of emergence from Doncaster Works in 1935 the first of the class — No. 2509 *Silver Link* — began work hauling the 'Silver Jubilee' in both directions daily, five days a week, for two weeks without any relief as no second engine of the class was yet ready. This duty required two 232 mile non-stop runs each day at an average speed of over 70 mph from start to stop. A beginning that holds no parallel whatsoever in the annals of a British steam locomotive and positive proof that when Gresley designed a locomotive all the necessary thinking and experimenting were over before it went out

onto the line to take up the duty for which it had been designed, with complete success and reliability.

With the A4 Pacifics Gresley had reached the pinnacle of achievement of a distinguished career. No. 4468 *Mallard* attained a world speed record for steam by attaining a speed of 126 mph and the class generally proved their competence on all types of duty from mundane freight haulage to tasks such as running the 'Flying Scotsman' with loads of some 550 tons from Grantham to King's Cross every day in even time. Later designs of Pacific were introduced by Gresley's successors but it was always to the A4 that the special duties were allocated. The experimental high speed run in May 1946, the Locomotive Exchange Trials of 1948, the introduction of the 'Elizabethan' non-stop express from London to Edinburgh in 1953 are examples and many others can be found.

So popular were these fine engines that no fewer than six of the original class of 35 have been preserved and some of these can be seen to this day performing on British Rail metals on a variety of steam specials.

This album is a pictorial tribute to the A4 Pacifics from their birth in 1935 to the late 1970s. Every facet of their power is graphically depicted.

NOTE:
ALL PHOTOGRAPHS CONTAINED IN THIS ALBUM THAT ARE NOT OTHERWISE CREDITED WERE TAKEN BY THE AUTHOR WHO WOULD LIKE TO THANK DR. JOHN COILEY AND JOHN EDGINGTON OF THE NATIONAL RAILWAY MUSEUM, YORK FOR THEIR VALUABLE ASSISTANCE IN MAKING AVAILABLE MANY OF THE EARLY PHOTOGRAPHS THAT APPEAR WITHIN THESE PAGES AND TO ARTHUR CAWSTON, MAURICE EARLEY, LES ELSEY, MIKE FOX, GAVIN MORRISON, BRIAN STEPHENSON, PHILIP WELLS, JOHN WHITELEY, TOM WILLIAMS AND JOHN P. WILSON FOR THEIR HELP IN PROVIDING PRINTS, NEGATIVES AND COLOUR SLIDES THAT WERE NOT AVAILABLE FROM THE AUTHOR'S OWN COLLECTION AND, WITHOUT WHICH, THIS ALBUM WOULD NOT HAVE BEEN POSSIBLE.

BIRTH OF A STREAMLINER

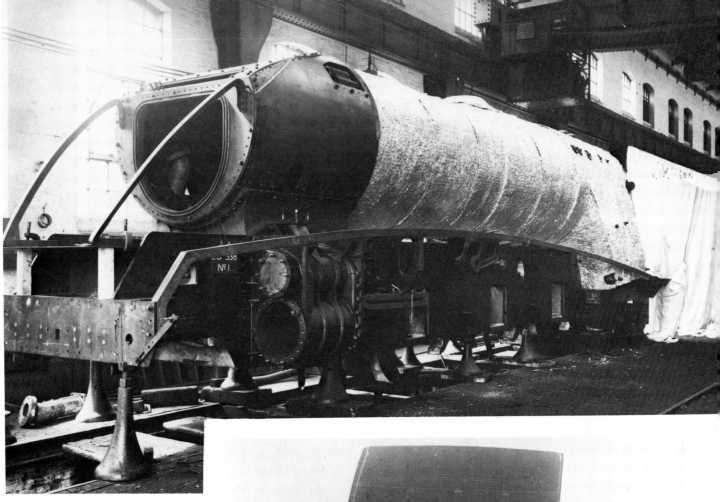

Plates 4-7: Official LNER photographs taken at Doncaster Works between July and September 1935 showing the construction of Gresley's first streamlined Pacific, No. 2509 *Silver Link*. Plate 7 shows the front of the casing opened to give a view of the access to the conventional smokebox door.

Courtesy National Railway Museum, York

Plates 8-9: The impressive front end and profile of *Silver Link* was enhanced by the most striking livery in three contrasting shades of grey. *Courtesy National Railway Museum, York*

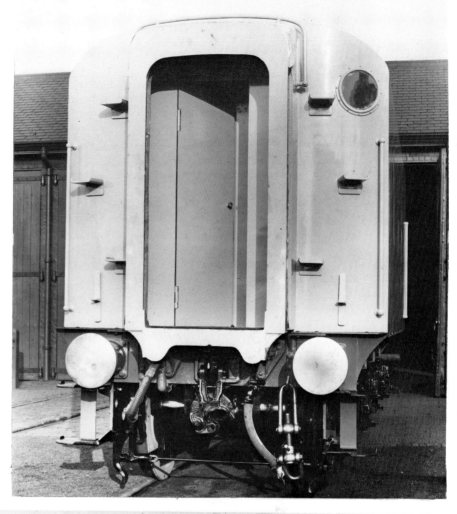

Plate 10: Corridor tenders had been in use on the LNER on some earlier Pacifics since 1928. Their success in allowing a change of locomotive crew during a long non-stop run was such as to have them fitted, with some modifications, to the first two batches of the Class A4. This official LNER photograph shows the door opening onto the corridor that ran the length of the right side of the tender and the vestibule connection and circular window in the upper right-hand corner.

Courtesy National Railway Museum, York

Plate 11: No. 2509 *Silver Link* climbs from Grantham with the 'Silver Jubilee' express in the summer of 1938.   *Rev. Arthur Cawston*

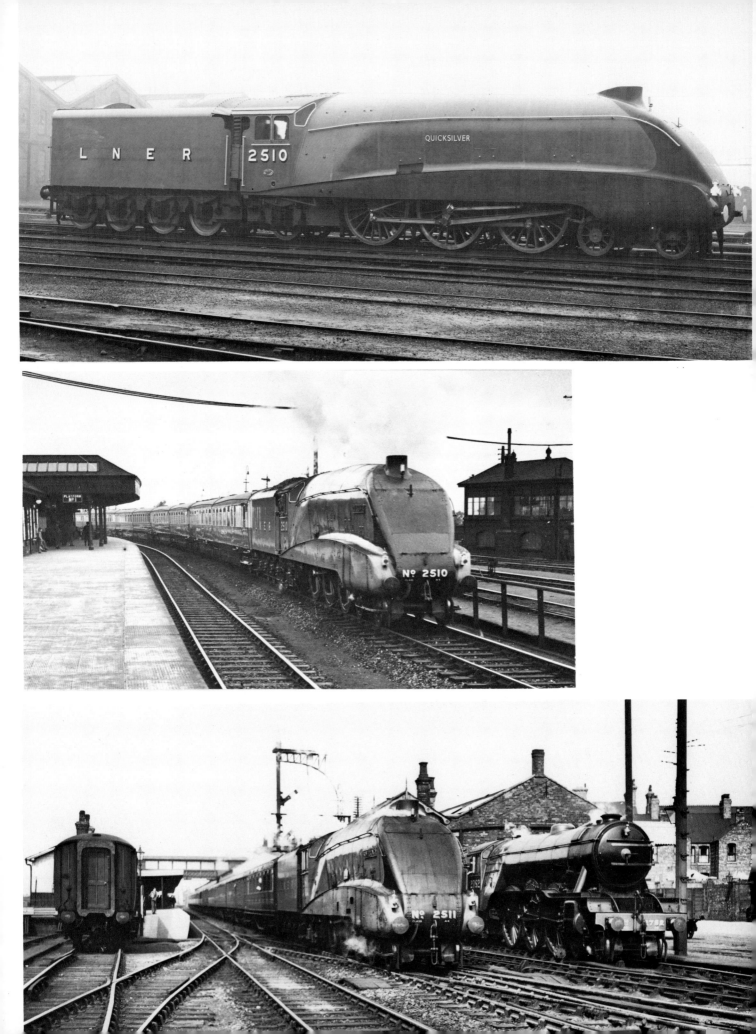

'SILVER' THEME CONCLUDED

Plates 12-16: Three further Class A4 Pacifics were turned out from Doncaster in 1935 to complete the first batch and their names continued the 'Silver' theme. No. 2510 became *Quicksilver*, No. 2511 *Silver King* and No. 2512 *Silver Fox*. The official 'profiles' were taken in September 1935 and 1936 respectively and show the original names painted in a central position on the streamline casing. Between November 1937 and May 1938, however, cast nameplates were fitted to all four and, in addition, *Silver Fox* also carried stainless steel replicas of a fox.

Shortly after leaving Edinburgh Waverley for King's Cross No. 2510 passes Portobello in July 1938 with the 'Coronation'. In April 1939 No. 2511 leaves Grantham for King's Cross with an express from Newcastle and passes A1 Pacific No. 2752 *Spion Kop* in the bay. No. 2512 is shown on Muskham troughs, Newark in June 1938 heading for Edinburgh with the down 'Coronation'.

Plates 12 and 16 Courtesy National Railway Museum, York
Plates 13 to 15 John P. Wilson

THE 'BIRD' NAMES APPEAR

Plate 17: No. 4482 *Golden Eagle* is posed for the official LNER photographer outside the Doncaster Plant where it had just been completed in December 1936. After the first four engines of the class it was the intention to name all the remainder with names of powerful British birds that were noted for their swift flight but, in the final analysis, only 23 of the class carried bird names and, ultimately, just 13 were to retain them to the end.

Courtesy National Railway Museum, York

Plate 18: No. 4486 *Merlin* bursts from Peascliff Tunnel, Grantham in June 1938 with the up 'Flying Scotsman'.

John P. Wilson

Plate 19: No. 4485 *Kestrel* moves a pre-war Aberdeen express away from a wet Edinburgh Waverley. This was one of the class to lose its bird name and in 1947 was re-christened *Miles Beevor* to honour one of the LNER top officials. *Kestrel* later appeared on a Peppercorn Class A1 Pacific.

John P. Wilson

Plate 20: No. 4487 *Sea Eagle* restarts the up 'Junior Scotsman' from Newark in September 1937. This name was also to finish up on a Peppercorn Pacific when the locomotive was re-named *Walter K. Whigham* in 1947.

John P. Wilson

Plate 21: No. 4464 *Bittern* with a King's Cross—Edinburgh express speeds through Northallerton in July 1938. The porter checking pigeon crates on the platform appears particularly unconcerned!

John P. Wilson

IN GARTER BLUE

Plates 22-25: Experience with the 'Silver Jubilee' express proving that the British public were prepared to pay for safe, high speed travel, the LNER decided to add to its prestigious streamlined trains and in July 1937 the 'Coronation' came into service to honour the Coronation of King George VI and Queen Elizabeth in that year. The bird names allocated to A4's Nos. 4488 to 4492 were changed to correspond to components of what was then the British Commonwealth and No. 4489, originally called *Buzzard* but changed before service to *Woodcock*, was altered again and emerged from the Plant in June 1937 painted in Garter blue with red wheels and carrying the name *Dominion of Canada*. This page shows the locomotive under construction in April 1937 and, as eventually turned out in June of that year with the arms of the country on the cab sides. Opposite is the cab of No. 4489 and a close up of the front end after a Canadian railway type bell presented by the Canadian Pacific Railway Company had been mounted in front of the chimney in March 1938.

Courtesy National Railway Museum, York

Plate 26: Before the bell was fitted
No. 4489 *Dominion of Canada*
hauling the down 'Coronation'
through New Barnet in north
London on 16th July, 1937.

John P. Wilson

Plate 27: No. 4492 *Dominion of New Zealand* speeds through Potters Bar in north London with
the up 'Coronation' in the summer of 1938.   *Rev. Arthur Cawston*

Plate 28: No. 4902 *Seagull* with the up 'Silver Jubilee' passes through York station in July 1938.
     John P. Wilson

Plate 29: In October 1937 the third streamlined train was introduced by the LNER to travel between King's Cross and Leeds. Given the title of the 'West Riding Limited' it was again the A4 Pacifics that were rostered for the duty and two of them were given new names suggestive of the Yorkshire woollen industry— No. 4495 *Golden Fleece* (originally named *Great Snipe*) and No. 4496 *Golden Shuttle*. Here the former approaches Wakefield Westgate with the up train on 20th July, 1938.   *John P. Wilson*

Plate 30: South of Edinburgh the up 'Flying Scotsman' approaches Portobello on 13th July, 1938 headed by No. 4489 *Dominion of Canada*.   *John P. Wilson*

ON SHED IN THE 1930's

Plate 31: When No. 4489 was re-named *Dominion of Canada* the name *Woodcock* was given to No. 4493, seen here on the turntable at Darlington just before the Second World War.   *Courtesy National Railway Museum, York*

Plate 32: The beautiful profile of No. 4492 *Dominion of New Zealand* at Doncaster in July 1937.
            Courtesy National Railway Museum, York

Plate 33: With a yard full of a variety of LNER locomotive power No. 4489, still named *Woodcock* at this
stage, displays its corridor-type tender showing the
original style of fairing at the front end of the coal space
and around the water filler.

Courtesy National Railway Museum, York

Plate 34: The 100th Gresley Pacific, No. 4498, is fittingly
named after Sir Nigel who is photographed beside the
locomotive in 1937.

Courtesy National Railway Museum, York

Plate 35: No. 4490 *Empire of India* approaches Grantham in September 1937 with a three coach local service for Peterborough. Although constructed for the crack expresses of the day the A4's sometimes found themselves rostered to a mundane duty such as this when more appropriate motive power was unavailable.   *John P. Wilson*

Plate 36: No. 4498 *Sir Nigel Gresley* speeds the 11.50 am from King's Cross through Claypole, south of Newark, in 1938.
                                                   Maurice W. Earley

PRE-WAR DUTIES

Plate 37: The up 'Flying Scotsman' headed by green liveried No. 4485 *Kestrel* approaches Hadley Wood in July 1937. Proving just as competent with the 500 ton, 52½ mph 'Flying Scotsman' as they were with the 220 ton, 70 mph 'Silver Jubilee' the general service batch of 17 engines constructed during 1936 were painted in standard passenger green livery as it was thought that a silver/grey livery would conflict with the varnished teak coaches that they would be required to haul.

Rev. Arthur Cawston

Plate 38: No. 4491 *Commonwealth of Australia* lifts the down 'Coronation' easily up the gradient to Potters Bar near Ganwick in 1937. *Rev. Arthur Cawston*

Plate 39: The final 14 locomotives of the class appeared in 1938 making a total of 35. By this time it had been decided that the Garter blue livery had proved more acceptable than either the silver grey or the green for the A4's and all of the first two batches were repainted accordingly with the final batch appearing from Works in blue. No. 4900 *Gannet* with the up 'Silver Jubilee' passes Great Ponton in 1938.

Rev. Arthur Cawston

THE 1938 BATCH

Plate 40: No. 4500 *Garganey* became *Sir Ronald Matthews* in March 1939 and is posed for the official LNER photographer outside Doncaster Works in that year.

Courtesy National Railway Museum, York

Plate 41: When this official photograph of No. 4468 *Mallard* was taken at Doncaster in March 1938 no one was aware of the fact that this locomotive was to become the most famous of the class and probably the best known anywhere in the world. For it was just four months later that the world speed record for steam traction of 126 mph was achieved.

Courtesy National Railway Museum, York

Plate 42: Ill-fated No. 4469 *Gadwall* approaches Grantham with the 'Flying Scotsman' in 1938. Renamed *Sir Ralph Wedgwood* in March 1939 this engine was to become a casualty of World War II (see Plate 47).

Rev. Arthur Cawston

Plates 43-45: In 1937 the LNER began experimenting with roller bearings in the axle-boxes of three of the A4 Pacifics, it being considered that they would require much less frequent service than the plain bearings and that their life mileage would be much higher. No. 2509 *Silver Link* was fitted with the Timken type, No. 4492 *Dominion of New Zealand* received Hoffmanns and No. 4493 *Woodcock* ran with the Skefco variety. The three types—in the order stated—are illustrated and, by pure chance, three different styles of lettering are also shown. Those with the Timken and Hoffmann variety retained them but those that were to be fitted with the Skefco type were part replaced by plain bearings again in 1958.

Courtesy National Railway Museum, York

Plate 46: For more than two years from when war was declared in September 1939 the A4's continued to be painted in Garter blue when going through works but from the end of 1941 this standard was no longer possible and they were painted black overall without lining. Still looking every ounce a thoroughbred No. 4496 *Golden Shuttle* was photographed at Doncaster in January 1942 after receiving the 'treatment'.

Courtesy National Railway Museum, York

Plate 47: No. 4469 *Sir Ralph Wedgwood* was damaged beyond repair by a German bomb at York on 29th April, 1942 reducing the class to 34 locomotives. The tender only was salvaged and was eventually fitted to Thompson Class A2/1 Pacific *Highland Chieftain* after being changed from vacuum to steam braking. It was withdrawn with this engine in 1960. The name *Sir Ralph Wedgwood* was transferred to No. 4466 *Herring Gull* in January 1944.

Courtesy National Railway Museum, York

Plate 48: Conditions that prevail during wartime bring about an inevitable deterioration in maintenance of all types. Time was an extremely valuable commodity and it was considered that it was being wasted by having to remove the skirting covering the motion and wheels of the A4's every time that attention to them was required. The first of the class to have the skirting removed was No. 4462 *Great Snipe* (later renamed *William Whitelaw*) although a form of panelling was restored forward of the cylinders before the locomotive went back into traffic. Still retaining blue livery the locomotive in this condition was photographed at Doncaster in June 1941. Later all the skirting was removed from the class during 1941/42 and they remained in this condition to the end. *Courtesy National Railway Museum, York*

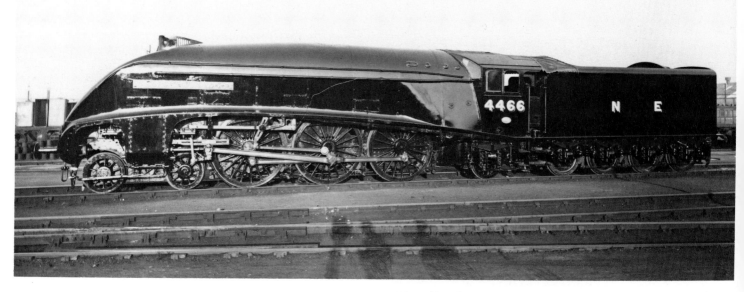

Plate 49: After receiving the new name of *Sir Ralph Wedgwood* No. 4466, newly repainted in wartime black livery and with the skirting completely removed, is posed for the official camera in January 1944.
Courtesy National Railway Museum, York

Plates 50-52: At the height of the war in August 1944 a strange ceremony of sorts was performed in the Works yard at Doncaster when No. 4486 *Merlin* in unlined black livery was temporarily renumbered and renamed on three successive occasions for the purposes of photographs being taken of the locomotive 'disguised' as No. 1928 *Brigid*, No. 1931 *Davina* and finally as No. 1934 *Bryan*. The temporary identity was affixed only to the left side of the casing and was removed before the engine returned to traffic. It later transpired that the numbers and names were the birth dates and christian names of the children of Mr. Fitzherbert Wright, then a new director of the LNER, who later had his own name affixed on a more permanent basis to Class B1 4-6-0 No. 61249!

Courtesy National Railway Museum, York

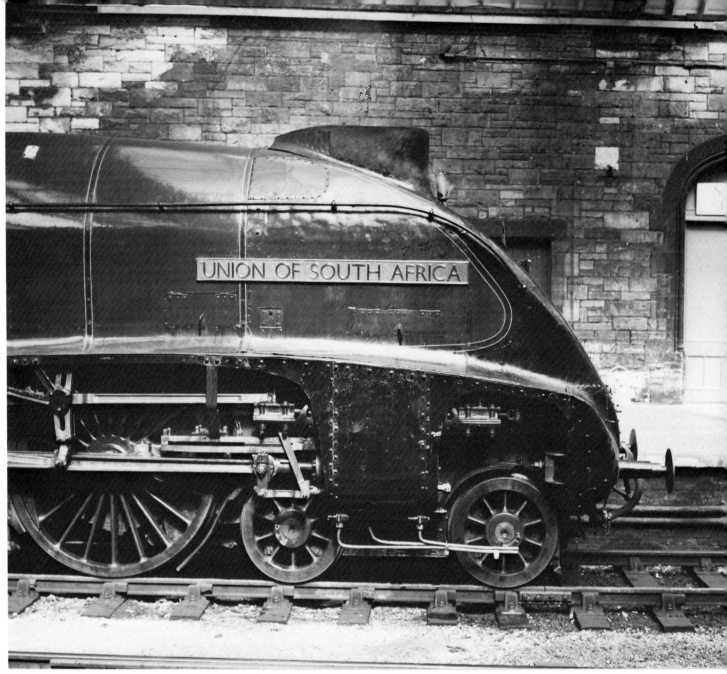

THE NAMES

LNER Original Number	Original Renumbering	Thompson Renumbering	British Rail Number	Original Name	Subsequent Name/s
4500		1	60001	Garganey	Sir Ronald Matthews
4499		2	60002	Pochard	Sir Murrough Wilson
4494		3	60003	Osprey	Andrew K. McCosh
4462		4	60004	Great Snipe	William Whitelaw
4901		5	60005	Capercaillie	Charles H. Newton Sir Charles Newton
4466	605	6	60006	Herring Gull	Sir Ralph Wedgwood
4498		7	60007	Sir Nigel Gresley	—
4496		8	60008	Golden Shuttle	Dwight D. Eisenhower
4488		9	60009	Union of South Africa	—
4489		10	60010	Woodcock	Dominion of Canada
4490		11	60011	Empire of India	—
4491		12	60012	Commonwealth of Australia	—
4492		13	60013	Dominion of New Zealand	—
2509		14	60014	Silver Link	—
2510		15	60015	Quicksilver	—
2511		16	60016	Silver King	—
2512		17	60017	Silver Fox	—
4463		18	60018	Sparrow Hawk	—
4464		19	60019	Bittern	—
4465		20	60020	Guillemot	—
4467		21	60021	Wild Swan	—
4468		22	60022	Mallard	—
4469		—	—	Gadwall	Sir Ralph Wedgwood
4482		23	60023	Golden Eagle	—
4483	585	24	60024	Kingfisher	—
4484	586	25	60025	Falcon	—
4485	587	26	60026	Kestrel	Miles Beevor
4486	588	27	60027	Merlin	—
4487		28	60028	Sea Eagle	Walter K. Whigham
4493		29	60029	Woodcock	—
4495		30	60030	Great Snipe	Golden Fleece
4497		31	60031	Golden Plover	—
4900		32	60032	Gannet	—
4902		33	60033	Seagull	—
4903		34	60034	Peregrine	Lord Faringdon

Plate 56: Carrying the new number 32, *Gannet* storms past Greenwood Box in April 1948 with a down express. The Great Northern Railway somersault signal is clearly in evidence.   *Rev. Arthur Cawston*

Plate 57: The famous Locomotive Exchanges took place in 1948 and, for the first time, A4's could be seen in action on the metals of the old GWR, LMS and Southern. No. 22 *Mallard* races through Sonning Cutting on the approaches to Reading on 26th April, 1948 with the 1.30 pm Paddington—Plymouth. This was a pre-test run in which the Gresley machine acquitted itself very well. *Maurice W. Earley*

Plate 58: On 28th April, 1948 *Mallard* was on Reading shed awaiting the relief crew to return her to King's Cross. *Maurice W. Earley*

Plate 59: Topping Camden Bank, out of Euston, in grand style No. 60034 *Lord Faringdon* heads the down 'Royal Scot' for Glasgow in May 1948 during the Locomotive Exchanges.

F.R. Hebron—courtesy Brian Stephenson

Plate 60: No. 60033 *Seagull* arrives at Waterloo on 11th June, 1948 with the 'Atlantic Coast Express' from Exeter.

F.R. Hebron—courtesy Brian Stephenson

Plate 61: Traversing Great Western metals at Reading No. 60033 *Seagull* heads westward with the 1.30 pm Paddington—Plymouth express on 28th April, 1948. It was probably no coincidence that the A4's selected by Doncaster for the Locomotive Exchanges were all of the type fitted with double chimneys! *Maurice W. Earley*

Plate 62: The post-war version of the 'West Riding' is headed by No. 60006 *Sir Ralph Wedgwood* and is shown near Hadley Wood in the spring of 1949. The first six coaches are pre-war streamlined stock. These streamlined trains ceased to operate immediately upon the outbreak of war and were never revived. *Maurice W. Earley*

Plate 63: No. 60007 *Sir Nigel Gresley* **emerges from Copenhagen Tunnel in April 1955 with a heavily laden 13 coach morning express for Leeds.**

Plate 64: No. 60015 *Quicksilver*, now fitted with a double chimney, has steam to spare tackling the climb up Holloway Bank towards Finsbury Park in April 1958 with an express for Hull. In fact, all the A4's had been fitted with Kylchap double blastpipes and chimneys by November 1958 and this move effectively solved the problem of poor steaming on some of the engines due to inferior coal.

Plate 65: No. 60010 *Dominion of Canada*, hauling a long express for Edinburgh, emerges from under the road bridge on the bank from Copenhagen Tunnel to Finsbury Park on a sunny November morning in 1953. Even in those days the London Transport bus proclaims that 'Daz washes whitest!'

Plate 66: No. 60015 *Quicksilver* passes the Finsbury Park carriage sidings in June 1953 with the down 'Norseman' for Newcastle (Tyne Commission Quay).

Plate 67: No. 60026 *Miles Beevor* hauls the down 'Northumbrian' express through Finsbury Park in April 1952. This was one of the many occasions in the 1950's when one express looked just like another as headboards, whilst provided in those days, often were not used.

Plate 68: No. 60025 *Falcon* emerges from the blackness of Copenhagen Tunnel into the summer sunshine of July 1953 with an express for Leeds.

Plate 69: An early morning relief express for Glasgow is made up of a motley collection of coaching stock
and is lifted up Holloway Bank in fine style by No. 60015 *Quicksilver*. This particular engine was allocated
to King's Cross (34A) in 1951 and remained a 34A locomotive until withdrawn in April 1963.

Plate 70: No. 60013 *Dominion of New Zealand*, with
twelve maroon coaches for Leeds and Bradford, climbs
towards Finsbury Park in fine style. Apart from two short
spells at Grantham (35B) and Haymarket (64B) this
engine was allocated to King's Cross for the whole of its
life. *Tom Williams*

Plate 71: This photograph of No. 60034 *Lord Faringdon*
was taken when the engine was allocated to King's Cross
in the early 1950's. When constructed as the last of the
class in 1938 *Peregrine*, as the locomotive was then named,
was first allocated to Doncaster (36A) where it remained
for four years. After a few months at King's Cross in 1942
it then went to Grantham for over five years and returned
to London in 1948 where it was a regular performer from
King's Cross until transfer to north of the Border in 1963.
The engine was finally withdrawn from Aberdeen Ferryhill
(61B) in August 1966.

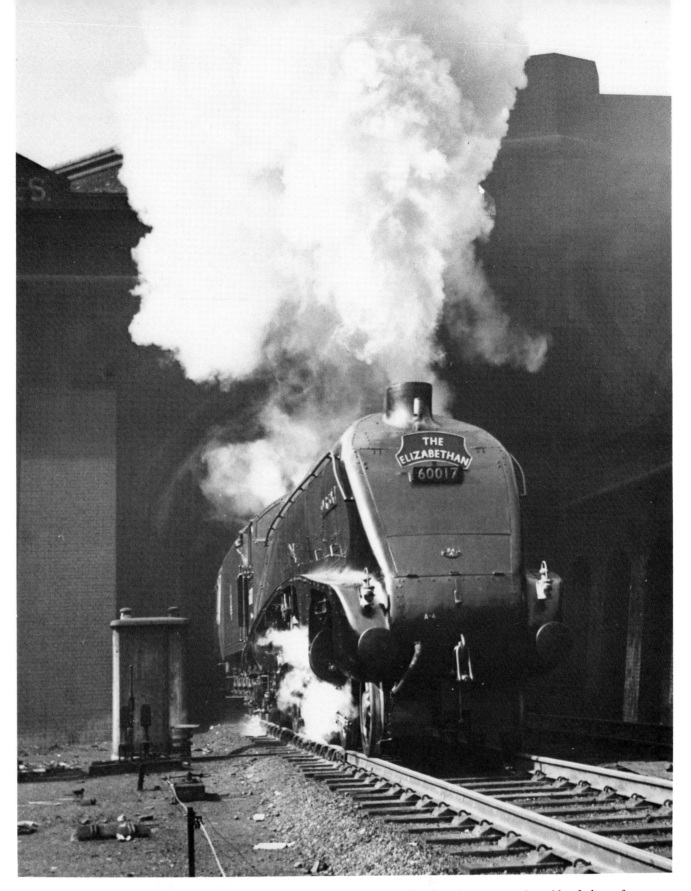

Plates 72-74: Once the war was over the LNER was quite sharp off the mark to restore the pride of place of their streamlined 'Pacifics' and from September 1945 the black livery started to be replaced with Garter blue. After some colour experimentation at Nationalisation the British Rail standard green livery was finally applied to all the class between 1951 and 1953 and, until the final days, the class was generally kept in good external condition by the various shed staff as can be witnessed by these three examples taken on Holloway Bank. No. 60003 *Andrew K. McCosh* heads the 9.40 am 'Norwegian Express' for Newcastle, No. 60025 *Falcon* steams easily up the adverse gradient despite a heavy summer express and No. 60017 *Silver Fox* bursts out of the tunnel with the 'Elizabethan' for Edinburgh, the express that took over the timings of the post-war 'Capitals Limited' after the Coronation of Queen Elizabeth II.

FREIGHT DUTIES

Plate 75: No. 60010 *Dominion of Canada* heads south through Wood Green in north London in July 1952 with a fitted freight for King's Cross yards.

Plate 76: Dominion of Canada climbs the gradient to Potters Bar in the early winter of 1951 with the famous King's Cross Yards—Niddrie 'Scotch Goods' and was a regular performer with this train during the early 1950's.

Plate 77: Another photograph of *Dominion of Canada* with the down 'Scotch Goods' seen emerging from Hadley Wood Tunnel. The correct terminology for this train should have been the 'Scottish Goods' as it never carried any of the 'hard stuff'. *Rev. Arthur Cawston*

Plate 78: No. 60013 *Dominion of New Zealand* with the 'Scotch Goods' makes a fine picture climbing Stoke Bank at speed. *Tom Williams*

THE PLANT CENTENARIAN

Plates 79-82: To commemorate the centenary of Doncaster Works in 1953 a number of special trains were run. Appropriately No. 60014 *Silver Link* was one of the locomotives involved and is shown here under preparation at King's Cross shed and later with the 'Plant Centenarian' at Belle Isle between Gasworks and Copenhagen tunnels just out from King's Cross.

Plates 83-84: No. 60034 *Lord Faringdon* receives attention at King's Cross shed in 1955 alongside Gresley Class V2 2-6-2 No. 60903 and Peppercorn Class A1 Pacific No. 60155 *Borderer* and, below, No. 60028 *Walter K. Whigham* awaits the next turn of duty with a Gresley Class A3 Pacific No. 60066 *Merry Hampton.*

Plates 85-86: In the company of an Ivatt Class J52 0-6-0ST and a Thompson Class L1 2-6-4T, No. 60003 *Andrew K. McCosh* awaits a path onto the King's Cross turntable before being backed down to the terminus to take out an Anglo-Scottish express in May 1955. A year earlier at Gateshead (52A) No. 60012 *Commonwealth of Australia* retires to the shed having brought in the up 'Flying Scotsman' from Edinburgh as far as Newcastle.

Plate 87: On a gloomy day in October 1954 No. 60005 *Sir Charles Newton* and No. 60008 *Dwight D. Eisenhower* are prepared for their next duties at King's Cross shed. A Class V2 2-6-2 and a Thompson Class B1 4-6-0 No. 61144 are also on view.

Plate 88: Two Gateshead allocated locomotives, Nos. 60001 *Sir Ronald Matthews* and 60020 *Guillemot* are attended to outside the home shed in August 1954. Apart from the one destroyed by enemy action during the war No. 60001 had the distinction of being the only one of the class to be allocated to just one shed for the whole of its existence. Gateshead first had this engine as No. 4500 *Garganey* in April 1938 and saw the last of it upon withdrawal in October 1964 when it was cut up by scrap metal merchants in Blyth, Northumberland.

ROYAL TRAINS

Plates 89-90: The Royal Train, conveying the Royal Family from King's Cross to York for the Duke of Kent's wedding on 8th June, 1961, approaches Essendine behind No. 60028 *Walter K. Whigham.* Just eleven days later another Class A4, No. 60003 *Andrew K. McCosh*, is again entrusted to Royalty and leaves Stamford for the return journey to Peterborough and King's Cross.   *Philip H. Wells*

Plate 91: With the fireman, seemingly, hard at work No. 60033 *Seagull* heads a down express near Beningborough, north of York in 1960.　　　　　*Gavin Morrison*

Plate 92: No. 60025 *Falcon* leaves Leeds Central on 2nd April, 1961 at the head of the 12.30 pm express for King's Cross.　　　　　*Gavin Morrison*

TITLED TRAINS AT WOOD GREEN

Plate 93: The up 'Northumbrian' comes through the station at Wood Green in April 1952 headed by No. 60003 *Andrew K. McCosh*.

Plate 94: No. 60024 *Kingfisher* passes Wood Green No. 4 signal box with the up 'Tees-Tyne Pullman' on the same day.

Plate 95: The down 'Heart of Midlothian' for Edinburgh passes Wood Green in March 1954 in charge of No. 60034 *Lord Faringdon*.

Plate 96: Heading a special parcels No. 60032 *Gannet* passes Ganwick, between the Potters Bar and Hadley Wood tunnels in July 1951.

Plate 98: No. 60019 *Bittern* makes a fine sight in the spring sunshine of 1950 heading the down 'Tees-Tyne Pullman' through Greenwood.

Rev. Arthur Cawston

Plate 99: At speed through the rebuilt Hadley Wood station in May 1962 No. 60014 *Silver Link* heads a down Leeds express.

Les Elsey

Plate 97: With time lost due to Sunday track maintenance No. 60008 *Dwight D. Eisenhower* fairly hurtles through the old Hadley Wood station with a down Leeds express that the driver intended to be on time at its destination!

Plate 100: Steaming so freely that Hadley North Tunnel, which it has just left, is still free of any smoke, No. 60030 *Golden Fleece* heads for King's Cross with an express from Leeds in 1953.

Plates 101-103: Three scenes taken at Greenwood in June 1950. On the left No. 60021 *Wild Swan* heads the 'Yorkshire Pullman'. Above No. 60013 *Dominion of New Zealand* is in charge of the 'West Riding' and below No. 60017 *Silver Fox* heads the 'Capitals Limited'. *Rev. Arthur Cawston*

Plate 104: Heading the down 'White Rose' through Hadley Wood station, No. 60030 *Golden Fleece*, rouses the echoes of a cloudy July morning in 1952.

Plate 105: No. 60014 *Silver Link* roars out of Hadley South Tunnel in 1950 with the down 'Scarborough Flyer'.
Rev. Arthur Cawston

Plate 106: No. 60007 *Sir Nigel Gresley*, rostered to the down 'Tees-Tyne Pullman' on 6th July, 1954, makes a fine sight storming through Hadley Wood station.

Rev. Arthur Cawston

Plate 107: With barely a trace of exhaust to betray the incline through Hadley Wood, No. 60033 *Seagull* heads a late evening express for Aberdeen in July 1952.

Plate 108: A London-bound express from Newcastle is bustled through Ganwick in 1951 headed by No. 60017 *Silver Fox.*

Plate 109: A winter sun highlights the down 'Heart of Midlothian' climbing through Oakleigh Park in February 1953 hauled by No. 60014 *Silver Link.*

Plate 110: Before the cutting at Potters Bar was widened for four tracks and the retaining walls built, No. 60024 *Kingfisher* hurries an up express towards the capital in September 1953.

Plate 111: From exactly the same position but facing in the opposite direction, just a few moments after the above photograph was taken, No. 60006 *Sir Ralph Wedgwood* heads a down Edinburgh express towards Potters Bar station.

Plate 112: Braking for an adverse signal, No. 60013 *Dominion of New Zealand* will need all its power to restart this 13 coach Harrogate express whilst on the up grade approaching Potters Bar.

Plate 113: No. 60011 *Empire of India* emerges from Potters Bar Tunnel in September 1953 with a down Bradford express made up of a variety of coaching stock.

Plates 114-115: After the widening of Potters Bar cutting No. 60015 *Quicksilver* heads north with a Harrogate express on 16th July, 1955 while No. 60032 *Gannet* proceeds in the opposite direction on the same day with a King's Cross bound express from Tyneside.

EAST COAST PULLMANS

Plates 116-117: Nos. 60007 *Sir Nigel Gresley* and 60006 *Sir Ralph Wedgwood* head north from London and pass Greenwood and Finsbury Park respectively with the 'Tees-Tyne Pullman' and the 'Yorkshire Pullman'.

Top photograph Rev. Arthur Cawston

Plate 118: No. 60003 *Andrew K. McCosh* makes a dramatic exit from Leeds in March 1962 with the up 'Yorkshire Pullman'.

Gavin Morrison

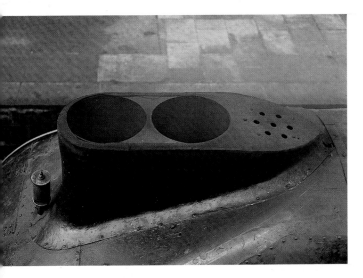

Plate 119: An unusual view of the double chimney fitted to No. 60009 *Union of South Africa*.

Gavin Morrison

Plate 119a: The *Silver Fox* embellishment fitted to both sides of the streamlined boiler casing of No. 60017. In fact, the fox was a stainless steel one!

Gavin Morrison

THE TUNNELS AT WELWYN

Plates 120-123: The two tunnels at Welwyn in Hertfordshire were popular places for photography although, personally, I was never blessed with decent weather conditions when visiting there with a camera. However, some reasonable results came about as shown on these two pages. No. 60013 *Dominion of New Zealand* storms out of the South tunnel into the short cutting between the two portals with a Saturday relief express for Leeds and Bradford and below this No. 60003 *Andrew K. McCosh* is travelling at about 80 mph emerging from the other end of the same tunnel with an express for the same destination. On this page No. 60007 *Sir Nigel Gresley* heads an express for Grantham from the South tunnel while No. 60008 *Dwight D. Eisenhower* has been rostered to the mundane task of hauling a Peterborough—King's Cross stopping train and has shut off steam for the Welwyn stop as it emerges from the North edifice.

TITLED TRAINS IN THE 1950's

Plates 124-128: In the immediate post-war years many regular services from King's Cross were honoured with a title and, at one time, no fewer than 15 trains carried a name. Being classed as the principal trains they were usually A4 hauled. No. 60003 *Andrew K. McCosh* on the difficult start from the London terminus at Holloway with the 'Norseman' for Newcastle (Tyne Commission Quay) is shown opposite together with No. 60028 *Walter K. Whigham* traversing Welwyn Viaduct with the down 'Heart of Midlothian' and No. 60032 *Gannet*, photographed overtaking a local service near Hornsey with the north-bound 'Flying Scotsman' in the spring of 1951. On this page 'The Capitals Limited' is whipped up Stoke Bank in effortless style by No. 60031 *Golden Plover* in August 1950 (*Rev. Arthur Cawston*) and No. 60009 *Union of South Africa* threads a path through Doncaster in 1954 with the up 'Elizabethan'.

Plate 131: Hauling the first part of the Ian Allan 'Pennine Pullman' from Marylebone to Sheffield on 12th June, 1956 No. 60014 *Silver Link* is photographed at Charwelton, between Woodford Halse and Rugby on the old Great Central Railway. *Tom Williams*

Plate 132: Passing Welwyn North station in 1953 No. 60010 *Dominion of Canada* heads an express for King's Cross.

Plate 129: Returning its 'White Rose' headboard to Holbeck for the following day's train, No. 60032 *Gannet* climbs away from Copenhagen Tunnel with a Leeds express in 1953. It was common practice to reverse the headboard in this way.

Plate 130: On the last lap into King's Cross No. 60022 *Mallard* coasts past Finsbury Park on the down grade with the 8.35 am from Glasgow on 13th May, 1954.

Plates 133-134: Bathed in early morning sunshine and with their clean green paint complementing the all maroon coaching stock Nos. 60032 *Gannet* and 60013 *Dominion of New Zealand* climb from King's Cross towards Finsbury Park with expresses for the north.

Tom Williams

Plate 135: With May sunshine glinting on its flanks No. 60034 *Lord Faringdon* heads the down 'Flying Scotsman' between Corby and Great Ponton on the southern approaches to Grantham in 1959.   *Tom Williams*

Plate 136: Haymarket based No. 60024 *Kingfisher* heads north with the 'Junior Scotsman' near Warkworth, Northumberland in 1951.   *Rev. Arthur Cawston*

Plate 137: A grubby No. 60025 *Falcon* prepares to leave Leeds Central on 15th June, 1963 with the very last steam-hauled 'White Rose'. This was also the last day for steam travel between Leeds and King's Cross.

Gavin Morrison

Plate 138: No. 60030 *Golden Fleece*, one of the two A4's named specially for the pre-war streamlined 'West Riding Limited', passes Holbeck High Level in October 1962 with the 1.55 pm from Leeds Central to King's Cross.

Gavin Morrison

Plate 139: No. 60020 *Guillemot* passes Beningborough, on the speed stretch north of York, in August 1961 with the up 'Heart of Midlothian'. By the early 1960's a number of the A4's were allowed to operate in a somewhat run down condition and, but for the post-war differences that are apparent, this photograph could almost have been taken in the early 1940's when the A4's livery was black!

Gavin Morrison

Plate 140: Heading a down express freight into Stoke Tunnel in July 1962 No. 60001 *Sir Ronald Matthews* is in slightly better external condition but the exhaust would seem to imply that all was not well on the inside!

Gavin Morrison

Plate 141: Taken from the buffer stops at King's Cross station it is journey's end for No. 60017 *Silver Fox* on 4th December, 1960. Three years later this historic locomotive was withdrawn and tragically cut up at Doncaster. Whilst the A4's are well represented among the preserved classes of locomotive it is particularly sad that this one should not have been among them.

Philip H. Wells

Plate 142: Even in the 1960's those of the class that were allocated to King's Cross (34A) were kept in quite good condition despite the advent of the new gleaming 'Deltic' diesels. In August 1962 No. 60015 *Quicksilver* climbs Holloway Bank with a down express.

Tom Williams

Plate 143: No. 60003 *Andrew K. McCosh* hares through the Lincolnshire countryside near Great Ponton in the spring of 1959 with an express for the north.
Tom Williams

Plate 144: Climbing Stoke Bank in an apparently nonchalant manner, No. 60007 *Sir Nigel Gresley* heads 12 coaches northwards in June 1962.
Tom Williams

Plate 145: On the final mile into King's Cross No. 60014 *Silver Link* rolls the 8.35 am express from Glasgow down the gradient into Copenhagen Tunnel on a sunny Saturday in May 1954.

Plate 146: With a London Transport trolley bus travelling along the Holloway Road above, No. 60017 *Silver Fox* heads the up 'Flying Scotsman' through the bridge on the King's Cross approaches on the same day.

Plate 147: No. 60015 *Quicksilver* approaches Welwyn North in 1954 with an express from Leeds for King's Cross.

Plate 148: No. 60028 *Walter K. Whigham* speeds through the Hertfordshire countryside near Hatfield with an up express in July 1962.
Tom Williams

Plate 149: Resplendent in green livery and steaming very freely, No. 60010 *Dominion of Canada* makes steady progress away from King's Cross towards Finsbury Park in August 1962 with a heavy express for Glasgow.

Tom Williams

Plate 150: The exhaust of No. 60025 *Falcon* beats down on the carriage roofs of a morning express for Cleethorpes in June 1953. The work-stained appearance was, happily, the exception in those days more than the rule.

SHINE AND GRIME

Plate 151: In immaculate ex-works condition No. 60030 *Golden Fleece* heads north through Hadley Wood in the summer of 1962.   *Tom Williams*

Plate 152: On a wet March day in 1952 No. 60021 *Wild Swan* races through Little Bytham with an express from Newcastle. The external condition of the locomotive was all that could be expected after a long journey on a day such as this.

BETWEEN DONCASTER AND SELBY

Plate 153: The world speed record holder, No. 60022 *Mallard,* south of Doncaster in August 1954 with the 11.25 am Leeds—King's Cross express carrying through carriages from Bradford and Ripon.

Plate 154: In May 1959 No. 60006 *Sir Ralph Wedgwood* heads away from Doncaster with the up 'Northumbrian' express.

Plate 155: A low evening sun highlights No. 60017 *Silver Fox* passing through Selby in 1958 with a King's Cross bound express from Newcastle.

Plate 156: On the same evening No. 60025 *Falcon* approaches Selby with the afternoon 'Talisman' express from King's Cross for Edinburgh Waverley. In the yards on the right a Thompson Class B1 4-6-0 shunts vans before leaving with a freight for Darlington.

AT SPEED . . .

Plates 157-158: A mere five coach express is treated with complete disdain by No. 60017 *Silver Fox* travelling fast through Hadley Wood in 1962 (*Tom Williams*) and, just 3 years earlier, No. 60022 *Mallard* races through Thirsk in Yorkshire with the down 'Flying Scotsman'.

. . . AND AT REST

Plates 159-160: No. 60007 *Sir Nigel Gresley* simmers at the buffer stops at Leeds Central on 28th February, 1960 with an express from King's Cross whilst No. 60020 *Guillemot* is coaled up and ready to go at Doncaster shed in March 1963.

Gavin Morrison

Plate 161: The 10 am Leeds—King's Cross express is taken past Beeston Junction on 5th June 1962 by No. 60033 *Seagull* and is already travelling at a 'fair rate of knots'.

Gavin Morrison

Plate 162: Travelling at nearly 100 mph the Locomotive Club of Great Britain's 'Mallard Commemorative Rail Tour' is headed by No. 60007 *Sir Nigel Gresley* on 6th July, 1963.

Philip Wells

Plate 163: Having brought in the up 'Heart of Midlothian' from Edinburgh No. 60016 *Silver King* prepares to come off the train at Newcastle Central to make way for an A1 Class 'Pacific' that will complete the journey to London.

Plate 164: No. 60032 *Gannet* rests on shed at Copley Hill (37B) in August 1961.   *Gavin Morrison*

ON SOUTHERN METALS

Plates 165-166: No. 60022 *Mallard*, with a special from Eastleigh to Swindon Works, passes Eastleigh West signal box in March 1965 and, below, is captured leaving Salisbury for Exeter in January 1963 with a Locomotive Club of Great Britain special.
Les Elsey

Plate 167: An A4 Preservation Society special approaches Allbrook in Hampshire in March 1966 headed by No. 60024 *Kingfisher*. This engine was allocated to Edinburgh St Margaret's (64A) at the time so had travelled a very long way to take charge of this train. Some six months later it was to be withdrawn.   *Clifford Elsey*

Plate 168: Another special in charge of No. 60022 *Mallard* moves away from Eastleigh carriage sidings heading all Southern malachite green stock.   *Les Elsey*

IN AND AROUND LEEDS

Plates 169-170: The 12.30 pm for King's Cross is eased away from Leeds Central in March 1961 in charge of No. 60021 *Wild Swan* whilst the 10 am Leeds–King's Cross, headed by No. 60006 *Sir Ralph Wedgwood*, steams past Beeston Junction, Leeds in June of the following year.

Gavin Morrison

Plates 171-172: For an A4 to be rostered for a local turn anywhere around the London area was almost unthinkable but, further north, the practice was not so uncommon and probably related to running in turns after attention at Doncaster Works. No. 60029 *Woodcock* and No. 60034 *Lord Faringdon* at Beeston Junction in June 1962 with Leeds to Doncaster locals have at least retained the dignity of express head codes!

Gavin Morrison

Plate 173: With steam to spare No. 60007 *Sir Nigel Gresley* departs from Stirling in August 1964 with the down 'St Mungo' express from Glasgow Buchanan Street to Aberdeen. By this time just seven of the class were still in traffic and all had been transferred to Scotland, from where they performed in fine fashion until the end of their days.
John Whiteley

NORTH OF THE BORDER IN THE 1960's

Plate 174: The 'West Coast Postal' was a regular turn for the A4's in Scotland during the 1960's. No. 60006 *Sir Ralph Wedgwood* leaves Stirling with the southbound train in April 1965.
John Whiteley

Plate 175: No. 60009 *Union of South Africa* heads the up 'Bon Accord' away from Stirling in 1965. This express had started at Aberdeen and was timed to arrive at Glasgow Buchanan Street in just three hours.

John Whiteley

Plate 176: No. 60034 *Lord Faringdon* moves the up 'Grampian' express away from Dunblane on 31st May, 1966 just a few weeks before being withdrawn from Aberdeen Ferryhill in August. *John Whiteley*

Plate 177: The up 'Grampian' is moved smartly away from Dunblane in August 1964 headed by No. 60027 *Merlin.*

John Whiteley

Plate 178: With steam issuing from just about everywhere that it shouldn't, No. 60024 *Kingfisher* heaves the southbound 'Grampian' express away from the mandatory Gleneagles stop in the spring of 1966.

John Whiteley

Plate 179: No. 60019 *Bittern* rolls the up 'Granite City' into Gleneagles in 1966.　　　*John Whiteley*

Plate 180: A really dirt encrusted No. 60026 *Miles Beevor* is given charge of the up 'West Coast Postal' and is caught by the camera passing Hilton Junction, Perth in August 1964.　　　*John Whiteley*

Plate 181: Seemingly in much better condition than when photographed in Plate 178 No. 60024 *Kingfisher* rounds the curve at Hilton Junction, Perth in April 1965 with the up 'Grampian'. *John Whiteley*

Plate 182: Another grimy A4 from the summer of 1964. No. 60034 *Lord Faringdon* emerges from Moncrieff Tunnel and approaches Hilton Junction with the southbound 'Grampian'. The last of the class to be constructed in July 1938 as No. 4903 *Peregrine* the locomotive lasted over 28 years and was withdrawn in August 1966. *John Whiteley*

Plate 183: The up 'Granite City' from Aberdeen arrives at Perth station in May 1966 where No. 60019 *Bittern* will take water. *John Whiteley*

Plate 184: On a balmy May night in 1966 No. 60024 *Kingfisher* arrives at Perth at 1 am with the 11 pm Glasgow–Aberdeen–a postal service that also provided passenger accommodation. *John Whiteley*

Plate 185: Begrimed but still looking every inch a thoroughbred No. 60031 *Golden Plover* departs from Perth in August 1965 with a Dundee to Glasgow express.   *Gavin Morrison*

Plate 186: No. 60019 *Bittern,* showing the locomotive class and allocated shed on the front in true Scottish style, arrives at Perth in June 1966 with an express bound for Aberdeen.   *John Whiteley*

Plate 187: Low, late evening sunshine highlights No. 60027 *Merlin* crossing the River Tay at Perth in August 1964 with a Glasgow to Dundee express.   *W.J.V. Anderson*

Plate 188: No. 60007 *Sir Nigel Gresley* moves the down 'Saint Mungo' away from Perth on the same day.   *John Whiteley*

Plate 189: Coaled, watered and ready to return to Aberdeen with one of the three hour expresses of the 1960's No. 60011 *Empire of India* is seen in the yards at Glasgow St. Rollox (65B) on a simmering August day in 1962.

Gavin Morrison

Plate 190: Leaving Perth for the south No. 60019 *Bittern* makes light work of the six coaches that formed the 'Granite City' express on 28th May, 1966.

John Whiteley

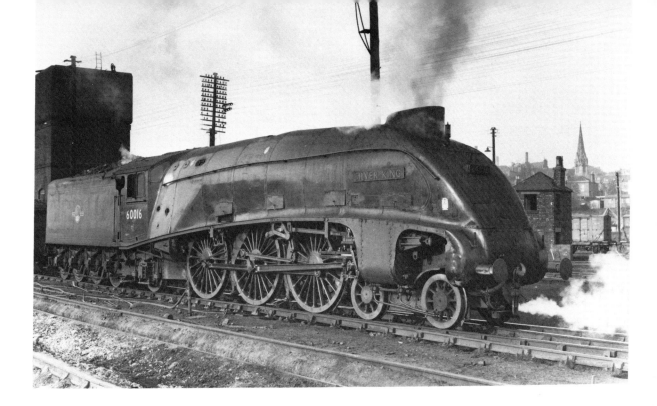

Plate 192: Just two A4's received the diagonal yellow stripe across the cab that signified that the locomotive was prohibited from working under the catenary on the electrified lines south of Crewe; No. 60031 *Golden Plover* and the example depicted here under repair at St. Margaret's Edinburgh (64A) in 1965, No. 60027 *Merlin*.

Les Elsey

FINAL DAYS

Plate 193: One month after withdrawal No. 60019 *Bittern*, stripped of shed and name-plates, is on York shed (50A) alongside Gresley Class V2 2-6-2 No. 60831 on 22nd October, 1966.

Gavin Morrison

Plate 194: On one of the very last workings of a Class A4 into London in October 1963 No. 60034 *Lord Faringdon* drifts down Holloway Bank with an express from across the border.

Plate 195: Although officially withdrawn in September 1966 No. 60019 *Bittern* heads a special for the Railway Correspondence and Travel Society on 16th July, 1967. Here the train departs from Beattock.

Gavin Morrison

Plate 196: Withdrawn in December 1962 No. 60014 *Silver Link,* the first of the class, awaits cutting up at Doncaster in the snows of February 1963. Whilst six of the class have been happily preserved it is considered a tragedy that this historic engine was not one of them.

Gavin Morrison

Plate 197: Although just a few weeks away from withdrawal No. 60003 *Andrew K. McCosh* is still entrusted to main line express duty and approaches Peterborough from the south on 19th November, 1962 with a fast for Leeds.

Philip Wells

Plate 198: With just over one year to go before coming face to face with the breakers' torch No. 60017 *Silver Fox* is in ex works condition in June 1962 heading away from Doncaster with an express for King's Cross that is made up of thirteen well filled coaches.

Gavin Morrison

Plate 199: No. 60006 *Sir Ralph Wedgwood* was one of the loco-motives whose life was extended when transferred to Scotland in 1963 and was not finally taken out of service until Autumn 1965. On one of the final turns whilst still allocated to King's Cross (34A) the engine heads the 12.30 pm to London from Leeds Central.

Gavin Morrison

Plate 200: Allocated to King's Cross from new in June 1938 No. 60033 *Seagull* spent all but four years at the London shed and was finally withdrawn from there in December 1962. Right up to the final days the engine was used on the King's Cross top link and just a few months before its demise is still considered good enough to tackle a very heavy Saturday morning express for Newcastle and the Tyne Commission Quay and has little trouble in haul-ing the load up the 1 in 107 out of the London terminus.

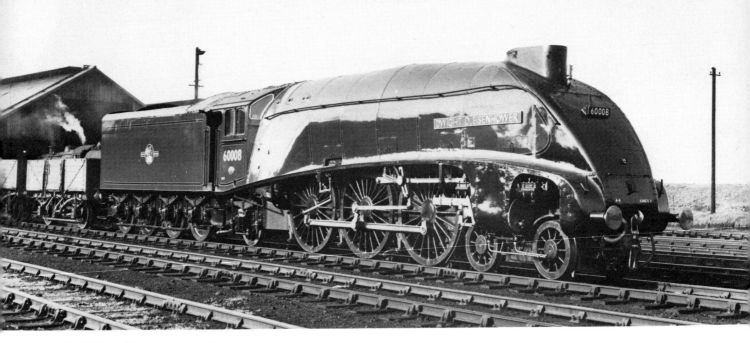

THE PRESERVATION SCENE

Plate 201: No. 60008 *Dwight D. Eisenhower* was completely overhauled at Doncaster Works after withdrawal from service in July 1963 and is seen here at Eastleigh shed (71A) in April 1964 on route for Southampton Docks where it was transported to the National Railway Museum of America in Wisconsin. Presented to them by British Rail this locomotive is generally considered as the finest preserved example of the class in its final form.
Les Elsey

Plate 202: Officially taken out of service two months previously No. 60019 *Bittern* is seen at Hexham, on the Newcastle to Carlisle route, with a special working in November 1966. *Gavin Morrison*

Plate 203: No. 60019 *Bittern* drifts down Beattock Bank with the RCTS railtour of July 1967 at Crawford.
John Whiteley

Plate 204: No. 60009 *Union of South Africa* heads south from Dundee and the River Tay and passes near Wormit with another Scottish special.
Mike Fox

Plate 205: A special organised by the north western branch of the Locomotive Club of Great Britain returns to Edinburgh from Dundee in June 1975 headed by an immaculate No. 60009 *Union of South Africa.*   *John Whiteley*

Plate 206: No. 4498 *Sir Nigel Gresley* heads away from Arbroath in June 1974 with the 'Tyne Dee Coastal' special, just one of the many 'Steam on British Rail' tours that have used A4 motive power in the 1970's.   *John Whiteley*

Plate 207: No. 60009 *Union of South Africa* emerges from the Moud tunnel and into the cutting through Princes Street Gardens, Edinburgh with the 'Forth & Tay' LCGB special in 1975.
Mike Fox

Plate 208: No. 4498 *Sir Nigel Gresley* with a 'Steam Safari' is photographed on the Newcastle–Carlisle line making light work of the modern, well filled coaching stock.
Mike Fox

Plate 209: After withdrawal in February 1966 No. 60007 *Sir Nigel Gresley* was purchased by the A4 Locomotive Society Ltd. who arranged for it to be completely over-hauled. Although no attempt was made to put the locomotive back into original appearance they did arrange for it to regain Garter blue livery, LNER on the tender and the number 4498. The engine in its present condition was photographed at Hereford.

Plate 210: Heading a special from Newcastle to York and back No. 4498 *Sir Nigel Gresley* crosses the King Edward Bridge at Newcastle in September 1975, a location that the engine saw frequently during service days.

John Whiteley

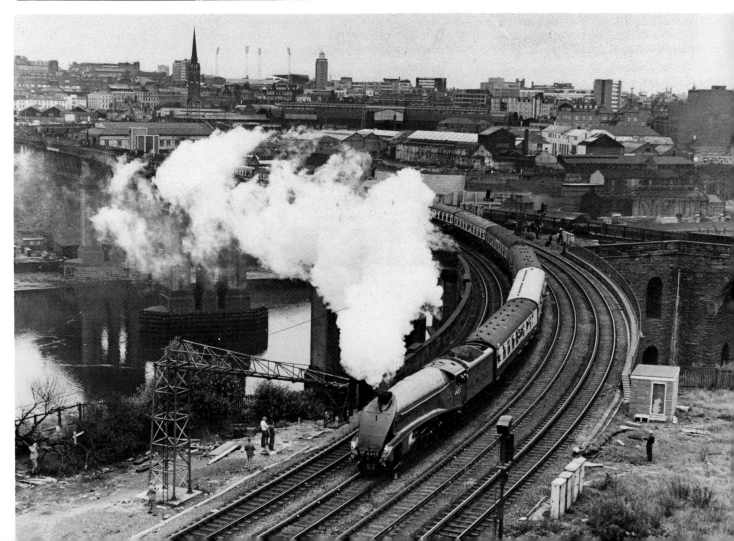

Plate 211: Heading the first leg of the 'Midland Jubilee' special from Chester No. 4498 *Sir Nigel Gresley* approaches Shrewsbury with a dozen well laden coaches on 1st October, 1977.

Plates 212-214: In pride of place inside the National Railway Museum at York No. 4468 *Mallard* displays the classic lines of a world record holder. Plaques to commemorate the achievement are affixed in a central position on the streamlined casing and were put there as a final flourish by the LNER just prior to Nationalisation in 1948.

Plate 215: On 29th October, 1977 No. 4498 *Sir Nigel Gresley* steams away from Skipton with the Carnforth to Leeds portion of the 'Pennine Venturer' special. This view clearly shows the beautiful restoration job by the A4 Locomotive Society.

Plate 216: Carrying the headboard of 'The Bon Accord' —one of the three hour Glasgow to Aberdeen titled trains that it once hauled with distinction — No. 60009 *Union of South Africa* steams on the Lochty Private Railway. *Mike Fox*

Plates 217-218: No. 60009 *Union of South Africa* crosses the Forth Bridge in May 1977 with the outward leg of the 'Silver Jubilee Special' from Kircaldy to Perth via Falkirk, Stirling and Dunblane.